Soundings from
An Empty Sea

Soundings from An Empty Sea

by

Matthew T. Cody

SOUNDINGS FROM AN EMPTY SEA

Donnaink Publications, L.L.C. 2014
Registered offices: 12750 Sophiamarie Loop, Orlando, FL 32828, United States
www.donnaink.org | (888) 564-7741

This is a work of adult fiction for persons over twenty-one (21) years of age. People portrayed in this work are fictional. Any resemblance to persons living or dead is coincidental. Any Web addresses/links contained within this book may have changed since publication and not be valid. Views expressed in this book are those of the author and do not necessarily reflect views of the publisher; hereby the publisher disclaims responsibility for them. All Rights Reserved to Publisher. This includes the right to reproduce this work in any form whatsoever without permission in writing from the publisher, except for brief passages in connection with a review.

This book is sold subject to the condition that is shall not, by way of trade or otherwise, be lent, resold, hired out, or otherwise circulated without the publisher's prior consent in any form of binding or cover other than that in which is published and without a similar condition including this condition being imposed on the subsequent purchase. The scanning, uploading and distribution of this book via the Internet or via any other means without the permission of the publisher is illegal and punishable by law. Please purchase only authorized print or electronic editions, and do not participate in or encourage piracy of copyrighted materials. Your support of the author's rights is appreciated. Safe Harbor as Appropriate.

For more information: bulk orders and/or marketing and promotions contact the Special Markets Division at special_markets@donnaink.org
12750 Sophiamarie Loop, Orlando, FL 32828

Editors: Philip Bartholomew, Quante Bryan, Shelby Catalano, and Dana Queen.
Cover Design: Sprinkles on Top Studios, Ms. Sarah Forster.

Copyright © Donnaink Publications, L.L.C. for Matthew T. Cody, 2014.

LIBRARY OF CONGRESS HAS CATALOGUED THIS TITLE AS FOLLOWS:
Cody, Matthew T.
Soundings from an Empty Sea / Matthew T. Cody
63 p. cm.
ISBN: 978-1-939425-66-9 (ack. pbk.); ISBN: 978-1-939425-99-7 (ack. digital)
[1) Literature, 2) Poetry, 3) Acrostics, 4) Relationships, 5) Adult, 6) Sexuality, 7) Erotic Poetry, 8) Bondage, 9) United States, 10) United States.)
Published in the United States of America; 12, 11, 10, 9, 8, 7, 6, 5, 4, 3, 2, 1.

TABLE OF CONTENTS

Table of Contents v

Preface xi

Acknowledgement xiii

Introduction xv

Abduction 1

ADDICTION 1

Adoration 2

Adrenaline 2

Altered State 3

Anime 3

Awakened 4

Bisexual 4

Behavior Modification 5

Blindfolds 6

Bondage 6

Bruise 7

Cages 7

Candles 7

SOUNDINGS FROM AN EMPTY SEA

ACROSTICS AND MORE

Chains	8
Chattel	8
Ckhooaass	9
CockMilking	9
Collar	10
Confinement	10
Consensual	11
Corset	11
Discipline	12
Dominant	12
Domme	13
Edging	13
Electrical play	14
Endorphins	14
Erotica	15
Feet	15
Femmedomme	15
Fishnets	16
Floggers	16
Flogging	17

MATTHEW T. CODY

ACROSTICS AND MORE

Forced Orgasm	17
Freckles	18
French Maids	18
Gagging	19
Gloves	19
Goddess	19
Gothic	20
Hands	20
High Heels	20
Hoods	21
Hunted	21
Hypnosis	21
Impact Play	22
Intelligence	22
Kidnapping	23
Kissing	23
Kneeling	24
Lace	24
Librarians	24
Lipstick	25

SOUNDINGS FROM AN EMPTY SEA

ACROSTICS AND MORE

Masks	25
Masks	25
Master	26
Mind Control	26
Mistress Ynhared	27
Mummification	28
MystressSyn	28
Nipples	29
Obsession	29
Pansexual	30
Passion	30
Photography	31
Riding Crop	31
Seduction	32
Sensation Play	33
Sensory Deprivation	34
Sex Magic	35
Shackles	35
Slavery	36
Sublime	36

MATTHEW T. CODY

ACROSTICS AND MORE

Submission	37
Surrender	37
Tears	38
Tempted	38
The Cross	38
Thorns	39
Tickling	39
Waxplay	40
Whip	40
About The Author	41
Visit the Author	43
Publisher Website	43
Facebook Fan Page	43
Twitter	43

PREFACE

"Soundings from an Empty Sea" are mostly acrostics regarding human relationships. Most relationships have arguments and most of the arguments are over trivialities. Unfortunately, most of the arguments escalate way out of proportion.

I believe that if one in the relationship makes the decisions, then the amount of stress or distress goes down and the amount of peace and pleasure goes up. As with all relationships, they are personal. Finding your puzzle piece or allowing each other to be transformed to fit takes work, but more so trust.

ACKNOWLEDGEMENT

There are people I would like to acknowledge but, unfortunately, the topics of these writings and open interest in them may lead to undesirable attention. Let it be known that I did have encouragement from some people and to them thank you.

INTRODUCTION

Greeting from the other side of the computer, I have always liked learning. Oddly, this made me drop out of high school and join the Navy as soon as I turned eighteen. It was a great experience, which permitted me to visit different countries, meet different people and experience different cultures.

Luckily, we are mostly the same, but the differences define us. When we interact in diverse circumstances we change them and they change us. I am that sum today and mostly the same, but different tomorrow.

I hope putting some of these differences on paper will enlighten, entertain and educate.

Soundings from An Empty Sea

ABDUCTION

A journey started, at dusk, alone.
Blacktop passing beneath my feet.
Darkness lives where the sun had shone.
Umber shadows line the street.
Car disabled, on the shoulder.
Two ladies are dressed for sin.
Impassive both, one young one older.
Offering help, with a shy grin.
Night befalls, as the needle goes in.

ADDICTION

Ambition narrowed down to One
Desire anchored to my core
Deeds requiring caution
Intoxication makes me explore
Crawling down to the dungeon
Terrified but You ensure
Induced to drinking some odd potion
Overpowering just like before
Nervous as You lock the door.

SOUNDINGS FROM AN EMPTY SEA

ACROSTICS AND MORE

ADORATION

Alone all day I think of you,
Dreaming what the future brings.
Obsessing over some issue,
Remembering those intense lashings.
Aching joints and black and blue,
Thinking of the cane that stings.
Intensely craving some taboo,
Of flogger thuds and a wand that sings.
Neck devices are like wedding rings.

ADRENALINE

Awareness at its apogee.
Desire marked by the glowing blush.
Rope and leather tether me,
Eager for the striking brush.
Needing to not be free,
Another stroke, my body's flush.
Lust as this does have a fee,
Intense pain does make you gush.
Nature's nepenthe makes pain flee,
Epinephrine is such a rush.

ALTERED STATE

Ambulating through mind and space.
Led around by a hidden guide.
Tracing threads, from place to place.
Examining facets, I try to hide.
Regressing toward my primal face.
Emotions that I'm strongly tied.
Dimensions, enlightenment tries to erase.
Senses, our ancestors had strongly relied.
Tacent tutors teaching grace.
Animal gifts are locked inside.
Time to join the human race.
Embracing natural primitive pride.

ANIME

Alluring forms with big round eyes,
Navy dresses with knotted ties.
Imagination that causes bliss,
Muliebral sims that blush and kiss.
Enthralling girls with margaric thighs.

AWAKENED

Aroused so slowly, feeling sick
Wondering why I'm in a jail
All a round are walls of brick
Keeling down and feeling pale
Eyeing iron bars so thick
No one ever posting bail
Entering Your high heels click
Doom and desire make me quail

BISEXUAL

Boy or girl is not the issue.
Intelligence and aesthetic frame.
Sensual in something see through.
Eager in the bedroom game.
Xenial and can subdue.
Undaunted and hard to tame.
Allured to acts that are taboo.
Lust from beauty is all the same.

BEHAVIOR MODIFICATION

Bells rang by Pavlov, made beasts drool.
Enlightening us, with how to train.
Harsh methods are, an effective tool.
Avoiding things that bring us pain.
Vapid thoughts, in a darkened pool.
Immersed in waters that restrain.
Orders given, soft and cool.
Receptive is our lonely brain.

Minutes, or months, may have past.
Ontology, has, no mark of time.
Dendrites making pathways last.
Inspiration, leads, to the sublime.
Finding joy inside this caste.
Ideals reached by tortured climb.
Chains of steel may hold me fast.
Attachments stronger change me to mine.
Taction links us steadfast.
Intertwined, our thoughts do chime.
Obsessive feelings have amassed.
Needful love is such a crime.

BLINDFOLDS

Blackness, is one's field of view.
Looking out, with other senses.
Intuition may give a clue.
Nervously, my body tenses.
Devoid of sight, aromas clearer.
Floral scents, I breathe in.
Olent aura, means you are nearer.
Light hot breath tickles my skin.
Dainty clicks of high heeled shoes.
Swish of leather, time to begin.

BONDAGE

Black as ink, I lay here waiting.
On my back, immobile wanting.
Never knew the things I'm hating.
Developed, into a lustful haunting.
Affixed, like a butterfly, on a pin.
Groaning into a drool soaked cloth.
Evenings like are this so full of sin.

BRUISE

Badge of honor earned through pain
Raw and sore though it may be
Ushered forth with Madam's cane
Ice could make the swelling flee
Since they hurt much to obtain
Erasing them is not for me.

CAGES

Crafted spaces, of detention.
Arresting those, demanding pleasure
Guarding ones, who dared to mention
Eccentric thoughts, extreme in measure
Sequestered 'till the torture session.

CANDLES

Colored wax, and a piece of string.
Age old instrument that scares the dark.
Nitid flame, makes people sing.
Discharging light so bright and stark.
Lucent lake does form a ring.
Erupting liquid, makes a mark
Seductively, You sooth and sting.

SOUNDINGS FROM AN EMPTY SEA

ACROSTICS AND MORE

CHAINS
Cold they feel when first attached.
Heat drawn quickly from the skin.
Already smoldering thoughts are hatched.
Intense dark feelings do begin.
Naked flesh, hardly scratched.
Smell of leather, time to begin.

CHATTEL
Connected to the Lady's lands,
Here to mind what needs attending.
Attachments stronger than metal bands,
Tasks and service seem unending.
Thoughtfully yielding to Her demands,
Evoking dreams of my ascending.
Longing for the heat that brands.

CKHOOAASS

Circles, and diamonds and squares at odd angles.
Kaleidoscope vistas, that looks quite insane.
Heavenscapes growing, out of knots and weird tangles.
Areas planer, those aren't real plain.
Abstract shapes mixing with crystals.
Over and over, it's never the same.
Observing the pieces, resolves most riddles.
Solving the teasing is both work and a game.
Start with the edges and work to the middles.

COCKMILKING

Coupled to a wooden table
O-rings holding body fast
Clever hands so very able
Knowing things from lessons past
Moving deftly and observing
Intensely reading signals given
Lady's skill is so unnerving
Keenly to her goal she's driven
Immured between her silken hands
Needing her to let me rest
Granting wishes are not her plans

SOUNDINGS FROM AN EMPTY SEA

ACROSTICS AND MORE

COLLAR
Circle with so many functions
Overlooked in crowded places
Leash can lead to these injunctions
Leather posture cradles faces
Adoringly they make conjunctions
Removing inhibitions traces

CONFINEMENT
Cages, cells or body bags
Often I do think of these
Naughty thoughts have brought me here
Forcing me to learn to please
Imagining all kinds of things
Nightmares become erotic dreams
Electricity or wood that stings
Making tears come out in streams
Every moment blurs to one
No hints to tell if it's day or night
Transformation should soon be done
(Trapped in lust just feels so right.)

CONSENSUAL

Ceding rights and what to choose.
Orders given to be obeyed.
Never One to abuse.
Sanity always displayed.
Even play that leaves a bruise.
Night of passions marks will fade.
Securely tied for You to use.
Urgent pleadings the gag forbade.
Aglow with how You enthuse.
Lash marks runes of our crusade.

CORSET

Curves the body against its will.
Orders the flesh, so deathly still.
Raising the breast as though were cast.
Stifles breath, she thinks it's her last.
Elegance, she's attained her best.
Treasure encased, within her chest.

Curves the body, against its will.
Orders the flesh, so deathly still.
Raising the breast. as though were cast.
Smoothes her curves, never out classed.
Elegance, she's attained her best.
Treasure encased, with in her chest.

SOUNDINGS FROM AN EMPTY SEA

ACROSTICS AND MORE

DISCIPLINE
Darkness, there are many kinds.
Including those that blind our minds.
Sabotaging, both deed and thought.
Crippling panic, leads to fraught.
Illumination from within.
Points the way to repent.
Learning through discipline.
If honestly and well meant.
Naked truth, is what you'll see.
Extract the toll that sets me free.

DOMINANT
Distrusting partners without cause.
Overstating one's own class.
Magnifying people's flaws.
Inciting every lord and lass.
Never question your own laws.
Arguing just to harass.
Now i know i ain't no saint.
Though you are a Dom'n'ai'nt.

DOMME

Deiform[1] You appear to me.
On a chair holding a key.
Musing thoughts, across Your lips.
Moiré robe and snake skin whips.
Envisioning things to make me plea.
You appear to me
On a chair holding a key
Musing thoughts across Your lips
Moiré robe and snake skin whips
Envisioning things to make me plea.

EDGING

Every touch, thickens the link.
Deft hands playing with their toy.
Gently urging, to the brink.
Increased pleasure, a baiting ploy.
Nails, teasing flesh, our breath in sync.
Gamboling fingers will freedom destroy.

---

[1] Deiform appearing like or shaped like a god.

ELECTRICAL PLAY

Energized nerves, starts to tingle.
Listen to the generator whine.
Electrons and air, start to mingle.
Causing tension down my spine.
Tied to the cross, with room to wiggle.
Restrained with leather, rope and twine.
Instantly sparks make me wriggle.
Cobalt bolts, nick this flesh of mine.
All at once I start to giggle.
Laughing now, is not a good sign.

Paling in Your radiance.
Lucent, from time to time
Arrested, and in a trance.
You're so good, it is a crime.

ENDORPHINS

Excitement can make it flow.
Narcotic angel from the pit.
During flogging, fast or slow.
Orgasm closer, with every hit.
Rising higher with every blow.
Pain and pleasure. kissed and bit.
Heated aura, skin aglow.
Inhuman sounds I do emit.
Nerves alight from head to toe.
Sex endorphins make me commit.

EROTICA

Ecdysiast enticements do ensnare.
Round red lips, and ebony hair.
Onyx eyes that pierce your own.
Thoughts and desires, mysteriously grown.
Imagining the heat of a velvet kiss.
Craving bonds, that bring bliss.
Arts gift this, if you dare.

FEET

Finely boned and nails of red
Enticing me to kneel and start
Eagerly I bow my head
To kiss your toes and heat your heart

FEMMEDOMME

Femimine nature does radiate.
Epitome, of my teenage dream.
Majestically, you designate.
Machinations complete Your scheme.
Expiation[2], beyond the gate.
Debt decreased with every scream.
Over time, the tide does change.
Mending hurts, relieving pain.
Molding me, You rearrange.
Ecstasy is the strongest chain.

---

[2] Expiation - the act of making atonement.

FISHNETS

Filaments, of fine silk twisted.
In knotted patterns, should not be.
Something that, she enlisted.
Helping her to ensnare me.
Never able, to be resisted.
Encasing flesh from toe to knee.
Tethered, lead unassisted.
Slave to thoughts you spin from me.

FLOGGERS

Floppy mop or tightly braided.
Leather caresser of my skin.
Oft times loved, and sometimes hated.
Grinding confessions from within.
Going 'til, the flogger's sated.
Eruption of pain, does begin.
Redressing acts, all related.
Slow the cadence, then start again.

FLOGGING

Fettered to a giant X.
Lady's hands, caress my back.
Opinable, so She corrects.
Guiding me with every crack.
Grabbing me, as She reflects.
Intensity in every thwack.
Needing this, as much as sex.
Givingly, She does attack.

FORCED ORGASM

Fixed fast with cuffs, and hempen rope.
Oak bedposts to keep me tethered.
Raspy tongue licks away all hope.
Conscious of limbs, that are tightly leathered.
Every touch, of your hungry lips.
Drives away my resistive will.
Objections cease, to your fingertips.
Raging needs make nectar spill.
Gasps and groans, and pleas to escape.
Arching back strains, but the lines are strong.
Sweat beaded brow and mouth agape.
Made to submit, doesn't feel wrong.

FRECKLES

Flawless flesh with dainty dapple.
Random fleck, a red brown dot.
Enticing as a fresh picked apple.
Caressing tongue, tastes every spot.
Kissing speckles, light and quick.
Leisurely licking, turns flesh hot.
Edging towards, what's wet and slick.
Steered by playing, connect the dot.

FRENCH MAIDS

Frilly lace of white on black.
Ruby lips, with sultry pout.
Efficiency, you do not lack.
Need fulfilled, without a doubt.
Cleaning things, you have a knack.
Hoovering, 'till it's all out.
Musty scent mixed with lilac.
Aura of one so devout.
It grieves me so, to have to pack.
Desiring she, who made me shout.
Sensing need, will drive me back.

GAGGING

Guilty of stealing this perverse treasure.
Amazed, that I had begged for this.
Gated lips, with ball and tether.
Growls emitted, sometimes a hiss.
Interleaving, pain and pleasure
Never far from the abyss.
Groans blocked by orb of leather.

GLOVES

Gentle stroke, or stinging slap.
Leather, latex or made of lace.
Over knees, across Your lap.
Velvet touch kisses my face.
Each light touch, or sudden snap.
Seeking hands that do embrace.

GODDESS

Graceful in all acts of life.
Opposition always, fades to black.
Deftly defeating mundane strife.
Divinity takes, You give some back.
Evoking moans, with a whip and knife.
Selectively wounding, You caress not hack.
Seductive skills, You do not lack.

GOTHIC
Grenadine clad, the color black.
Ombré aura and blood red lips.
Torturing one, upon the rack.
Hewing with Your favorite whips.
Immortality, You may lack.
Ceasing life as red blood drips.

HANDS
Holding things the mind has made.
Allowing taction that can persuade.
Nails that play with nerves 'till frayed.
Divining desire, in scenes well laid.
Staying when the act's been played.

HIGH HEELS
Highly polished and made of leather.
Icon, of the feminine.
Geometrically put together.
Holding treasured flesh within.
Heralding all, to bow forever.
Echoes cause a compelling din.
Erotic beat like a drummer.
Leading me to unknown sin.
Strangely my loss feels like a win.

HOODS

Hiding all of sound and sight.
Over head and face, laced so tight.
Only thoughts, and touch are freed.
Desperate in my carnal need.
Seeking things that hide from light.

HUNTED

Hearing sounds, from some direction.
Umbral wells concealing peril.
Noises causing my detection.
Thought turning dark and feral.
Ensnared, subdued by an injection.
Delivered for intense correction.

HYPNOSIS

Hearing words, that sooth my senses.
Your voice comes from all directions.
Pendant sways, past my defenses.
Neurons making strange connections.
Oral proposals, erotic pretenses.
Suggestions leading to moral deflections.
Inviting pleasure, my body tenses.
Seeing my future in Your eye's reflections.

IMPACT PLAY

Incredibly, hanging all alone, suspended by cuff and chain.
Measured strokes, meted out, decorate my unmarked skin.
Paddles of wood, make me shout, give a stinging pain.
Applied in such, a caring way, that brings me back here again.
Canes sizzles, fiery hot, leaving well placed, well-earned welts.
Tawse strikes so fast and loud, producing painful piercing yelps.
Pulse is rising with the strop, and every strike of the riding crop.
Lashes from the cat-o-nine, makes me whine and squirm and hop.
All at once it's at an end, You stop, this special kind of play.
You kiss my neck from behind, I'm glad I came today.

INTELLIGENCE

Interweaving interaction.
Naked truth, may lead to passion.
Thought and reason, rule this faction.
Terrifying tool, of tactic taction.
Evolved in my souls extraction.
Learning from axonal action.
Leveraging, my id's attraction.
Increasing knowledge through inspection.
Guided thoughts, a chain reaction.
Evokes basal primal reflection.
Newly forced, forms of flection.
Clearly, You are my distraction.
Entirely to Your satisfaction.

ACROSTICS AND MORE

KIDNAPPING

Kissing You, seems rather strange.
In that my lips, are kind of numb.
Did You, somehow, arrange,
Narcotics so I would succumb?
Are those blinking lights hypnotic?
Pleasure runs throughout my veins.
Pain becomes oh so erotic.
Incessant teasing, whips and chains.
Needed fear and the exotic.
Gone is power, no will remains.

KISSING

Keenly touching each other's skin, with moist and trembling lips.
Intensity, matched with restrain, to make the moments last.
Sliding tongue, across Your neck, Your breast and soft curved hips.
Sucking mouth draws in Your flesh, holding firm and fast.
Intoxicating, you are so, from head to Your toe tips.
Nectar leaking from Your flower, I know my will won't last.
Give me leave, to drink from You, in swigs or nips or sips.

KNEELING
Kissing hugging stroking healing.
Not right now, but maybe after.
Eyes held down while thoughts are reeling.
Eventually, there will be laughter.
Listening to, high heels a-clicking
In a room devoid of din.
New thoughts fly, like whip tips flicking.
Goddesses, are made of sin.

LACE
Light thread tied, daintily.
A knotted aura, half hides Your face.
Casting shadows, gracefully.
Enticingly, it does encase.

LIBRARIANS
Ladies in glasses, heels and tweed.
Entrusted with tasks of power and knowledge.
Balancing on ladders, tending books that we read.
Receivers of stares, in town, school or college.
Although they are dressed so prim they succeed,
Reining in thoughts, and corseted cleavage.
Inducing dark thoughts, of things that we need.
Alone at her desk with "Of Human Bondage".
Noting the ones, whose eyes have curtseyed,
Succubus feed, on those that pay homage.

LIPSTICK

Laminates of every color and hue.
In hard smooth tubes, such a pleasure to bear.
Protecting flesh, so soft and so true.
Succulent treasures, encased with great care.
Textures so coaxing, will passion ensue?
Inviting to taste, if you would, but dare.
Caution crumbles, willpower's through.
Kissing her lips, she does ensnare.

MASKS

Molded plastic, feather, paint.
Abandoned virtues, of a wayward saint.
Second skin, of lies and lust.
Knowing secrets, broken trust.
Shows who we are or who we ain't?

MASKS

Maidens sometimes, head out to sea.
Alone with thoughts, while doing tasks.
Seeking whom, they ought to be.
Ketch and sails and room to bask.
Serenity, removes the mask.

MASTER

Makes me do things unfair.
Always knows when I'm not trying.
Spanks my ass, and pulls my hair.
Touches gently, to stop my crying.
Enthralling me, with after care.
Revives my soul, and leaves me sighing.

MIND CONTROL

Memories, are they false or true?
Inside my head is such a mess.
Nebulous thoughts all lead to You.
Deferring actions, relieves all stress.
Contradicting, makes me feel blue.
Orders received, I try to impress.
Nightly treatments, until tattoo.
Tactic commands, a lover's caress.
Raptly waiting, for the next cue.
Obedience, obsess, success.
Love is diving in the abyss for You.

MISTRESS YNHARED

Maker of things divine.
Intricate enclosures, of satin and lace.
Seams made strong, that do entwine.
Tape measure ensures, the size and place.
Ribbons so soft, materials fine.
Epitome, of style and grace.
Seductively clothed, will make others incline.
Swaying their minds, and starting the chase.
Yielding until, their thoughts do align.
Nurturing desires, that lead to a place.
Hunger develops, by sheer design.
Allowing the hunter, to set the pace.
Radiance approaching, nearly sublime.
Earthbound immortal, from this time and space.
Dressing this lovely, is surely a crime.

ACROSTICS AND MORE

MUMMIFICATION

Many times it goes around.
Until the body, disappears.
Movement stops, when fully bound.
Mind set loose, imagination, rears.
Igniting thoughts, walls burning down.
Forced to focus, your hopes, your fears.
Inducing ghosts of touch and sound.
Clinging desires, of many tiers.
Arousal evident, to those around.
Taut fabric allowing, taunts and leers.
Impotent to prevent, predators surround.
Obliged to sail to new frontiers.
Navigating this vessel, to shores profound.

MYSTRESSSYN

Margaric[3] sheen upon Your skin.
Yearnings spread, to those enthralled.
Solicitations, cause a din.
Trails mark from where, they have crawled.
Ruby lips, in a sardonic grin.
Eager supplicants come when called.
Smiling while sipping vin.
Slighted suitors, are appalled.
Still, spurned slaves try again
Your voice and laugh instills recall.
Nothing matches the original, Syn.

---

3   Margaric is pearl like.

NIPPLES

Numinous adornments, topping the breasts.
Impelling ascension, of the mound.
Pacing the climb, kiss by kiss.
Placing lips, at the top, evokes such a sound.
Licking your flesh, attaining such bliss.
Ecstasy emanates, all around.
Such perfection is joyful, where ever it's found.

OBSESSION

On command, to serve my quest.
Bowing to acknowledge Thee.
Subtle actions, are the test.
Every moment observed by me.
Seconds tic, time overstressed.
Senses searching hungrily.
Investigation, at its best.
Owned by this singularity.
Now enslaved, and obsessed.

PANSEXUAL

Passion, lust and total trust.
An open mind, though discerning.
Nudist, Buddhist or upper crust.
Someone agile to share a berthing.
Eloquence and keen interest.
Xenophiliac, with constant playing.
Uninhibited, and unbiased.
Alien, or perhaps an earthling.
Love and lust, the best conquest.

PASSION

Power contained, but not controlled.
Arousing dark thoughts, such a distraction.
Smothering logic, with hard kisses, bold.
Straining for frantic, raw carnal action.
Imagining flesh, to lick, suck and hold.
On rumpled sheets, rope helping your traction.
Nightmares and dreams, our desires abstraction.

PHOTOGRAPHY

Playing shadows, dark and deep.
Highlights brightening up the shot.
Objects cherished, chosen to keep.
Time ensnared, so not forgot.
Observing life, shallow and deep.
Grains like sand will tell the tale.
Reflections, impressions of consciousness seep,
Arranging patterns, as light waves do trail.
Puppies that grow, and willows that weep.
Histories stored, ignored and veiled.
Yesterday's dreams in coffins to sleep.

RIDING CROP

Rods so slender, and alluring.
Imagination, speeds ahead.
Dreams of what I am enduring.
Involving pain, and stripes of red.
Never knowing, what i'd be needing.
Galliardly. the stick has sped.
Confessing things, i should be hiding.
Revealing secrets, kept in my head.
Overtures of me abiding.
Passionately, i have pled.

SEDUCTION

Sub-rosa entwined, within every flower.
Easing the prey inside the maze.
Delicately guiding, with subtle power.
Understanding shown, with every phrase.
Carefully leading, with gentle suggestion.
Taking the time, to trip the trap.
Irrevocably insuring, total possession.
Onward they go, a gentle snap.
Not everywhere, can be found on a map.

Sub-rosa entwined in everything flowered.
Easing the prey, inside the maze.
Delicately guiding, you're subtly powered.
Understanding shown, with every phrase.
Carefully leading, with gentle suggestion.
Taking the time, to trip the trap.
Irrevocably insuring, total possession.
Onward they go, a gentle snap.
Now naked and begging, to be devoured.

SENSATION PLAY

Silence echoes inside my head,
Expanding to the unseen walls.
Naked standing, arms stretched and spread.
Smelling the leather, that installs,
Arousal laced, with an addictive dread.

Teasingly, I hear her foot falls,
Inviting clicks, make me see red.
Often things, that one recalls,
Nightmares born, from things unsaid.

Pain and pleasure, simply enthralls,
Lashes lovingly do embed,
Aches and stings, and kiss that falls,
Yearning for you, so deeply I've bled.

SENSORY DEPRIVATION

Surrounded by silence, as far as the eye can see.
Enveloped in darkness, that weighs so heavily.
Not hot nor cold though, chills run insides me.
Smells of memories, to keep me company.
Observing nothing, my consciousness starts to fray.
Randomly, remembering, things i'd never say.
Yearning to find what i am, and what i am not.
Dissolving my ego, the goal of someone's plot.
Ebbing until the tide is dead low.
Programming me to be apropos.
Revising the thing that i used to be.
Inventing something, that's no longer me.
Vaguely thinking, this one is aware.
Absent is it, who used to be there.
Taking in beauty, truly profound.
Implicitly and totally, irrevocably bound.
Owned forever now, unconditionally.
Never wishing, to be free.

SEX MAGIC

Senses sharpened through carnal pleasure.
Energy mounts with every thrust.
Xenogenous talisman, of middling measure.
Mounting me, with spikes of lust.
Awakened power, the looked for treasure.
Granted to those, who truly trust.
Invoking pleas, to aid this quester.
Channeling power, while gagged and trussed.

SHACKLES

Smooth and shiny, cool on the skin.
Heavenly, heavy metal rings.
Always anchoring, secret thoughts.
Chain links perfect, exquisitely wrought.
Keys of silver, hidden away.
Left here waiting, until it's time to play.
Every day it's always the same.
Smiling widely when hearing my name.

SLAVERY

Solitude, for time un-ended.
Listlessly curled on the floor.
Agonizing over every task.
Voices chill me to the core.
Echoing footsteps, coming nearer.
Ringing of keys unlocking the door.
Yearning for this, contentment depended.

SUBLIME

Stunning beauty, upon a throne.
Ubiquitous, is Your charm.
Bewitching looks, with hair windblown.
Loveliness, does disarm.
Ink black eyes and high cheekbones.
Mesmerizing, provides the balm.
Erasing memories, of the pain and harm.

SUBMISSION

Sapphire dreams, stimulate the allusion.
Unlocking the cause of this condition.
Baring the reason for constant confusion.
Motivated by Your permission.
Instructions unheeded, bring a contusion.
Studying Your needs, is my mission.
Sub-ordinance may end my seclusion.
In a house of Victorian Tradition.
Only hoping, this is no delusion.
Naked and kneeling, please accept this petition.

SURRENDER

Strong-willed, or so i'd thought.
Urges for Your touch make me,
Realize what life has brought.
 Roaming lonely, though i'm free.
Endless battle, my mind is fraught.
No one to hear my silent plea.
Doubtless, i am caught,
Evermore on bended knee.
Relinquishment, is what i sought.

TEARS

Teeming face to floor.
Earnings for Her physical chore.
Atonement can't be paid in cash.
Rectified, with cane and lash.
Submitting to whom, i adore.

TEMPTED

Thinking You hear my every thought.
Echoing all around my head.
Mesmerized, fearing i'm caught.
Poised to hear what You just said.
Taction feared, as well as sought.
Entranced, wishing, to be led.
Dungeon, kitchen, bath or bed.

THE CROSS

Two pieces of wood, a simple design.
Hanging from them are cuffs of leather.
Eventually, I will get the sign.
Crawling to my physical tether.
Reaching up, for the umpteenth time.
Outstretched, trying to calm my mind.
Soon the crosses, will pay for the crime.
She may be cruel but She's not unkind.

THORNS

Tracing the ridges, of my fingertip.
Hearing its whisper, when scraping the skin.
Over the crests, it deflects with a skip.
Running and dancing, until it digs in.
Nicking the flesh, oh so sharp and so quick.
Sorry, it whispers, for being a prick.

TICKLING

Trepidation, apprehension.
Insecure, and filled with tension.
Comprehension, no protection.
Kissing my exposed erection.
Lubrication, then flirtation.
Interrogation, stimulation.
No expectation of ejaculation.
Giggling madly, my violation.

WAXPLAY

Well timed drops, of tinted torment.
Achingly, the mind does wander.
Xanadu forms, from this foment.
Peace and pleasure, over yonder.
Lying still, throughout these travels.
Arrested, pain, makes me ponder.
Yielding makes my mind unravel.

WHIP

Whispering, slithering out of sight.
Heat and hurt, from any direction.
Incisions or welts with every bite.
Pain becomes, a painful erection.

ABOUT THE AUTHOR

Matt Cody spends most of his time wandering. Looking for puzzle pieces that fit. The puzzle is himself. In-between searching there reading and cooking and baking.

Eventually, when he at least find the boarder pieces, he will settle down to fill in the body. These are the works of a future Bed and Breakfast Owner. Enjoy!

VISIT THE AUTHOR

PUBLISHER WEBSITE

DonnaInk Publications, L.L.C.: www.donnaink.org or www.donnaink.com

FACEBOOK FAN PAGE

https://www.facebook.com/AuthorMattCodyLinkedIn

TWITTER

@AuthorMCody

www.ingramcontent.com/pod-product-compliance
Lightning Source LLC
Chambersburg PA
CBHW070656050426
42451CB00008B/372